State Arts Agencies 1965–2003

Whose Interests to Serve?

Julia F. Lowell

Supported by

The research in this report was produced within the Enterprise Analysis division of the RAND Corporation. The research was supported by a grant from The Wallace Foundation.

Library of Congress Cataloging-in-Publication Data

Lowell, Julia F.
State Arts Agencies 1965–2003 : Whose Interests to Serve? / Julia F. Lowell.
p. cm.
"MG-121."
Includes bibliographical references.
ISBN 0-8330-3562-2 (pbk.)
1. Art commissions—United States—Finance. 2. U.S. states—Cultural policy. 3. Government aid to the arts—United States. I.Title.

NX740.L68 2004
700' .79'73—dc22

2004000925

Cover design by Eileen Delson La Russo

Published 2004 by the RAND Corporation
1700 Main Street, P.O. Box 2138, Santa Monica, CA 90407-2138
1200 South Hayes Street, Arlington, VA 22202-5050
201 North Craig Street, Suite 202, Pittsburgh, PA 15213-1516
RAND URL: http://www.rand.org/
To order RAND documents or to obtain additional information, contact
Distribution Services: Telephone: (310) 451-7002;
Fax: (310) 451-6915; Email: order@rand.org

Preface

State arts agencies throughout the United States now provide more than half of all public-sector funding for the arts and culture. In fiscal year 2000 alone, they sponsored over 2 million artists and almost 16,000 nonprofit arts organizations nationwide. Recognizing the importance of these agencies, The Wallace Foundation launched the State Arts Partnerships for Cultural Participation (START) initiative in 2001. START is designed to help state arts agencies develop new and more effective strategies for encouraging participation in the arts and culture in their states. As part of START, Wallace chose 13 state arts agencies to receive multiyear grants totaling $9.6 million to support programs, research, and outreach efforts on arts participation, including leadership training, pilot demonstration projects, and improved technical assistance.

A goal that has grown out of the START program is to identify, collect, and disseminate broad strategies that could strengthen state arts agencies' ability to serve state residents. To achieve this goal, the RAND Corporation is conducting a four-year study aimed at documenting and analyzing how state arts agency efforts to increase public participation in the arts may also be helping them to

- Find common ground about what sort of art should be publicly funded;
- Respond to taxpayers' desire for efficient and effective government; and
- Demonstrate the value of what they do to the residents of their states.

Together with partners at RMC Research Corporation, the RAND research team visited all 13 state arts agencies participating in START to conduct interviews and informal focus groups with agency directors and staff. The team also reviewed documents describing how the START agencies, as well as other state arts agencies, have changed their organizational structures, policies, and practices over the years.

This is the first in a series of short publications that will report on the study's findings and it reflects circumstances as of fall 2003. It is meant to set the context for the series by broadly describing the political evolution of state arts agencies from the 1960s to the present, and by identifying programs, policies, and approaches that may form the basis for new and more robust roles and missions.

This publication was produced within the Enterprise Analysis division of the RAND Corporation. The research is being supported by The Wallace Foundation as part of its continuing effort to help create and promote new standards of practice for arts and cultural organizations and funders that enhance broad participation in the arts. To promote that objective, The Wallace Foundation supports the development of knowledge from multiple sources and differing perspectives.

The RAND Corporation Quality Assurance Process

Peer review is an integral part of all RAND research projects. Prior to publication, this document, as with all documents in the RAND monograph series, was subject to a quality assurance process to ensure that the research meets several standards, including the following: The problem is well formulated; the research approach is well designed and well executed; the data and assumptions are sound; the findings are useful and advance knowledge; the implications and recommendations follow logically from the findings and are explained thoroughly; the documentation is accurate, understandable, cogent, and temperate in tone; the research demonstrates understanding of related previous studies; and the research is relevant, objective, independent, and balanced. Peer review is conducted by research professionals who were not members of the project team. RAND routinely reviews and refines its quality assurance process and also conducts periodic external and internal reviews of the quality of its body of work. For additional details regarding the RAND quality assurance process, visit http://www.rand.org/standards/.

Contents

Figures and Tables

Figures

Table

Summary

The early 2000s have been difficult for many, if not most, state and jurisdictional arts agencies (referred to as state arts agencies, or SAAs). In fiscal year (FY) 2003, a record 43 of 56 SAAs reported year-over-year declines in the general fund appropriations budgeted to them by their state legislatures. In FY 2004, 34 agencies reported further budget reductions, with nine of them—in California, Colorado, Guam, Florida, Michigan, Minnesota, Missouri, Oregon, and Virginia—reporting cuts of more than 30 percent. Six SAAs—those in Alaska, Arizona, California, Colorado, Missouri, and New Jersey—faced serious threats of elimination.

The immediate cause of these early-2000s budget problems is a fiscal crisis that, in many states, is unprecedented. However, as this report argues, these cuts to state arts budgets are more than just a one-time response to fiscal crisis by state officials. Findings from in-depth interviews with staff from 13 SAAs and a review of the literature on SAAs and the National Endowment for the Arts (NEA) suggest a growing mismatch between the grantmaking role and structure of many SAAs and the cultural and political realities they face. And even though many SAAs are trying to reach beyond their traditional grantee constituencies, the perception—if not the fact—that SAAs primarily serve artists and arts organizations rather than the broader public is yet to be overcome. A short review of the history of SAAs helps to explain why this is so.

The Early Years

Our nationwide system of SAAs was conceived by the founders of the NEA in large part because of their need to appease those who feared the creation of a dominating, European-style "Ministry of Culture." To win over these opponents, the federal-state arts partnership was created as a key provision of the NEA's enabling legislation. States wanting to receive federal arts money had to establish their own arts agencies and fund them through state legislative appropriations. However, at least at the beginning, the state-to-federal-dollar match in most states was considerably less than one-to-one. In fact, the lure of federal money was the primary reason most SAAs were established.

The consequences of the NEA's catalytic role in developing state-level support for the arts were somewhat paradoxical. Although the federal-state partnership's purpose was to offset possible cultural domination by Washington, D.C., there was no strong, positive vision for what the SAAs themselves should be. The result was that, like the NEA, most early SAAs operated under certain "elite" assumptions:

- The arts can be categorized into high and lesser art forms—that is, a strong distinction between "art" and "culture" can be made;
- The arts, and most of all the high arts, greatly benefit Americans as individuals and as a society;
- Support for "great art" should be the first priority of government because not enough great art will be created if support is left to the private market.

Many, though not all, states tended to translate these assumptions into support for high arts institutions (symphony orchestras, opera companies, ballet companies, art museums, etc.) rather than for artists or community-based arts organizations. Further, these assumptions formed the basis for a top-down, "If we build it, they will come" approach to public arts funding that was driven by the interests and priorities of arts aficionados rather than the general public. In many states, a political *quid pro quo* was established in which the leadership and friends of major arts institutions agreed to lobby for their SAA's budget in return for a steady flow of grants.

The Populist Revolt

For the first ten years or so after the NEA was founded (1965), this top-down approach achieved successes on several fronts: State legislative appropriations for SAAs kept growing, new nonprofit arts organizations spread rapidly around the country, and many more Americans participated in arts events. By the mid- to late 1970s, however, populist critics of SAA policies were raising issues that resonated in state capitols. They argued that:

- Significant, even transcendent artistic endeavors originating from cultural communities outside the mainstream of American art were being ignored;
- Most Americans were not taking advantage of government investments in geographically dispersed high arts organizations; and
- In seeking to support only "the highest and the best," arts agencies were taking a too limited view of the ways in which Americans can benefit from the arts.

Responses to these criticisms differed across states. Many SAAs made significant programmatic changes, such as introducing folk arts and "expansion arts" grant programs that targeted rural and minority ethnic communities. Many also either introduced or directed more resources toward programs for community-based artists and for arts education. Several SAAs decentralized, either on their own initiative or because of legislative mandates, setting aside funds to be regranted through networks of local agencies. Between 1975 and the early 1980s, decentralization programs were adopted in Maryland (1975), Minnesota (1976), North Carolina (1977), New Jersey (1978), New York (1978), Massachusetts (1979), Virginia (1979), California (1981), and Michigan (early 1980s).

But although most SAAs greatly expanded their definition of the arts, and many allowed greater local control over grantmaking, SAAs as a whole continued to focus on arts production rather than consumption. And the political impact of the changes they introduced was disappointing: Local arts councils received much of the credit for regrants run through the budgets of decentralized agencies, and community-based artists and arts organizations did not turn out to be an effective lobbying force. At the same time, many of those who believed firmly that preserving and nurturing the high arts should be an arts agency's first priority began losing their faith in SAAs.

A Loss of Support

A drop in the NEA's basic state grants—combined with a severe nationwide recession—put SAAs under significant budgetary pressure in the early 1980s. SAA managers then looked to their major arts institutions for political support, only to find it had been eroded by the funding strategies they'd pursued in the 1970s as well as the broad cultural and demographic changes taking place in their states. Most members of the leadership (and audience) of the majors were either unable or unwilling to undertake significant lobbying efforts for their SAAs. Many turned to lobbying for line items for their own institutions rather than working for increases to their SAAs' overall budget.

Because of the breakdown of the *quid pro quo*, a number of SAAs sought support from the statewide citizen arts advocacy groups that, not coincidentally, were springing up around the country in the late 1970s and early 1980s. But SAAs soon recognized that these groups did not always share their priorities. Regardless of the original impetus for their founding, many of these groups came to be dominated—if not controlled outright—by large arts organizations that fiercely resisted SAA attempts to shift funds in other directions. Coalitions between small and large organizations often proved unstable.

The national economic recovery and the consequent restoration of state budgets in the mid-1980s once again allowed SAAs to straddle the ideological gap between the populist vision of funding diverse artistic expression and the elite vision of giving grants to encourage artistic excellence. But SAAs realized that total reliance on the major arts institutions for political support was no longer a viable strategy. Therefore, most SAA leaders worked hard to reach out to the increasingly culturally diverse populations within their states—without abandoning their major constituents. Their success varied, but they nonetheless found it hard to convince state legislators that their constituents—still primarily, if not exclusively, actual and potential grantees—represented the citizenry at large.

New Realities

Debates in the 1990s over what artists should or should not do with public money created even more political turmoil than had rocked SAAs in the 1970s. SAAs also suffered at this time because of state fiscal crises deeper than any they had collectively seen before. Many SAA managers thus began exploring ways to convince average citizens and their elected representatives that the arts were important to their lives—and that their SAAs were important to the arts.

SAAs realized that success entailed accounting for two new realities of American cultural and political life. First, the dominance of the "great art" rationale for public support of the arts—and the relative importance of the major high arts institutions in American society and American politics—had clearly diminished. No longer was there consensus on how public arts money should be spent. Second, government agencies had to be more responsive to voter interests and more able to demonstrate the results of their efforts to the public.

Further, SAAs had to begin grappling with the problem of their near-irrelevancy to their states' political establishments. The supply-side strategy of supporting arts producers had turned many SAAs into cash machines, but without much clout—and often without much money. Evidence from New Jersey, Ohio, and other states suggests that artists as well as average citizens often do not even know their state *has* an arts agency. This suggests that most people perceive SAAs as, at best, peripheral to their needs—and therefore expendable.

Looking to the Future

By almost any measure, SAAs have supported a tremendous number of people and organizations dedicated to making and presenting art. In FY 2000 alone, SAAs sponsored the work of over 2 million artists and almost 16,000 nonprofit arts organizations. Nevertheless, many SAA managers in the 2000s have become convinced that their agencies must undergo profound philosophical changes in orientation if they are to thrive rather than merely survive from year to year.

A large part of The Wallace Foundation's State Arts Partnerships for Cultural Participation (START) initiative now entails helping the START agencies think through new or refocused missions that will stand on more solid and enduring political foundations. An important first step is to recognize that each SAA's ultimate constituency comprises all its state residents, not just the state's community of arts aficionados, artists, and nonprofit arts organizations. As public servants, SAAs must strive to invest public resources in the arts institutions, activities, and artists that produce the greatest value for the people of their states. The heart of the initiative is a shift in SAA focus and funding from bolstering arts providers to serving people and communities. The 13 START agencies are working to put this idea into practice, but important issues remain, some which will be explored in later monographs in this series.

Acknowledgments

I greatly appreciate the continuing contributions of RAND Corporation colleagues Laura Zakaras and Elizabeth Ondaatje, who participated in many of the interviews and all of the discussions connected with this work. Many thanks also to M. Christine Dwyer and Susan Frankel of RMC Research Corporation, and to Kelly Barsdate, Director of Policy, Research and Evaluation at the National Assembly of State Arts Agencies (NASAA). Their extensive experience with state arts agencies, program planning and evaluation, and data collection in the arts has been a tremendous source of insight.

Kimberly Jinnett and Ann Stone of The Wallace Foundation helped guide the direction of the research and, with Lee Mitgang, made many useful suggestions that were adopted. Michael Kammen of Cornell University, John Kreidler of Cultural Initiatives Silicon Valley, and Anthony Radich of the Western States Arts Federation provided thoughtful critiques of an earlier version of this monograph. Jeri O'Donnell's careful editing improved the text. Finally, many thanks to all those who met with us at the Arizona, California, Connecticut, Kentucky, Massachusetts, Minnesota, Mississippi, Montana, New Jersey, North Carolina, Ohio, South Carolina, and Washington state arts agencies and took the time to describe their organizations and activities. The findings and recommendations presented here are solely those of the author.

CHAPTER ONE

Introduction

In fiscal year (FY) 2003, 43 of 56 state and U.S. jurisdictional arts agencies (SAAs) reported year-over-year declines in the general fund appropriations budgeted to them by their state legislatures (National Assembly of State Arts Agencies [NASAA], 2002).[1,2] Six SAAs—those in Alabama, California, Colorado, Iowa, Massachusetts, and Virginia—saw their legislative appropriations cut by more than 20 percent. In FY 2004, 34 SAAs experienced further budget reductions, nine of them—California, Colorado, Guam, Florida, Michigan, Minnesota, Missouri, Oregon, and Virginia—reporting cuts of 30 percent or more (NASAA, 2003). Attempts to shut down SAAs in Alaska, Arizona, California, Colorado, Missouri, and New Jersey failed in the end, but not without gaining considerable political support. In California, for example, an FY 2004 budget that would have zeroed out the California Arts Council was supported by the governor and would have passed the senate but for three votes. Ultimately, this SAA's legislative appropriation was cut by almost 90 percent.

The immediate cause of the state arts budget crisis in California and elsewhere is an unprecedented state fiscal crisis. According to the National Conference of State Legislatures (2003), states have struggled over the past three years to close a cumulative budget gap approaching $200 billion. Three out of four states have chosen to cut expenditures during this time of turmoil, with SAAs—along with other agencies dependent on discretionary state general funds—proving particularly vulnerable to the budgetary axe.[3]

[1] Both the state and the jurisdictional arts agencies are referred to as state arts agencies. The six U.S. special jurisdictions are American Samoa, the District of Columbia, Guam, Puerto Rico, the Northern Mariana Islands, and the Virgin Islands.

[2] Unless otherwise specified, legislative appropriations cited in this paper do not include line items.

[3] Lack of comparability of state budget data makes it difficult to assess the relative performance of SAAs in state budget battles. But certainly the arts have fared worse overall than, for example, education or corrections. In FY 2004, state general fund spending on higher education is budgeted to decrease by 2.3 percent, while spending on primary education and corrections is budgeted to increase by 2.3 percent and 1.1 percent, respectively (National Conference of State Legislatures, 2003). General fund spending on the arts, in contrast, is expected to decline by over 20 percent in aggregate (NASAA, 2003).

This report's position is that the state arts budget cuts of the early 2000s are not merely a one-time response to fiscal crisis by state officials. Information gathered from in-depth interviews with staff from 13 SAAs; from attendance at statewide, regional, and national arts policy conferences; and from the literature on SAAs and the National Endowment for the Arts (NEA) suggests that these cuts reflect a mismatch between the historical mission, role, and structure of many SAAs and the cultural and political realities they now face.[4] Another finding is that budget cuts made in the 1990s and 2000s have encouraged many SAAs to significantly rethink what they should be and do.

Why care about SAAs? One reason might be the magnitude of their grants. For example, in FY 1999 alone, SAAs provided approximately $250 million in grants to performing, visual, literary, and media arts organizations and artists; to schools, libraries, and social service providers; to correctional institutions, health care institutions, and religious organizations; and to other government agencies. This compares to roughly $50 million in grants provided by the NEA and almost $500 million in grants provided by state, county, and municipal governments through local arts councils (NASAA and NEA, 2001; NEA, 2000; Cohen, 2002).[5]

Nevertheless, when compared to the approximately $11 billion in private-sector giving to the nonprofit arts, culture, and humanities over the same period—let alone the amount Americans spend on for-profit arts and entertainment—spending on the arts by the American government at all levels is very small.[6] More important than the magnitude of the SAAs' monetary expenditures, therefore, is their role in determining whether and what sorts of arts and cultural activities are funded with taxpayer dollars. In principle, all allocations of public money to the arts should be guided by broadly agreed public purposes of the arts and culture. But, as argued below, the historical political consensus on what those public purposes are and how to achieve them has broken down. SAA thinking about how best to build a new consensus—or how to operate without one—could bring about the most important shift in the nature of direct U.S. government funding of the arts since the NEA's founding in 1965.

This document is the first in a series of monographs reporting the findings of a RAND Corporation study of the changing missions and roles of SAAs. While the study covers all of the 56 SAAs, many of the examples are drawn from the 13 SAAs that have received multiyear grants from The Wallace Foundation.[7] Originally, Wallace's

---

[4] The interviews, which took place between between April 2002 and July 2003, were conducted as part of The Wallace Foundation's State Arts Partnerships for Cultural Participation (START) initiative. The 13 START states are Arizona, California, Connecticut, Kentucky, Massachusetts, Minnesota, Mississippi, Montana, New Jersey, North Carolina, Ohio, South Carolina, and Washington.

[5] Author's calculations. SAA grant figures net out regrants to local arts councils; NEA figures net out regrants to the states through the State Partnership Agreements.

[6] Calculation based on data from Grantmakers in the Arts, 2001, and AAFRC Trust for Philanthropy, 2000.

[7] Summary descriptions of the 13 SAAs that received these grants are in Appendix A. Summary descriptions of the other 43 SAAs are in Appendix B.

State Arts Partnerships for Cultural Participation (START) initiative was designed to help SAAs develop new and more-effective strategies for increasing public participation in the arts. Cultural participation is still at its core, but the initiative has evolved to include the missions and roles of SAAs—and ways of demonstrating to state residents, and to state political leaders, that SAAs deserve continued public support.

This report traces the evolution of SAAs since their inception in the 1960s, charting their search for appropriate and politically sustainable missions and roles. Findings from in-depth interviews with staff at the 13 START agencies and from the small body of published literature on SAAs are used to highlight distinct phases in SAAs' historical development. Also shown is how current SAA programs and emphases grew out of historical attempts to reconcile differing views on what constitutes the highest value of the arts to a democratic society.

Additionally, the report describes the evolution in thinking taking place in the START agencies, and documents some of the resulting changes in their approaches to political leaders, the arts community, and the public. These changes include more-active efforts to engage with political leaders and the public, a sharper focus on core missions, more strategic grantmaking, and, perhaps, a shift away from the grantmaking role toward a complex combination of roles that may better serve their state residents.

The report concludes with issues likely to be key to the success of the new approaches to political leaders, the arts community, and the public. These issues, almost certainly to be addressed differently in different states, are all possible topics for future monographs in this series.

CHAPTER TWO

The Early Years: SAAs and the NEA Model of Support for the Arts

Children of the NEA

Our nationwide system of SAAs was conceived by the founders of the NEA, all of whom were informed and inspired by three arts policy milestones of the late 1950s and early 1960s: W. McNeil Lowry's Ford Foundation arts program, Nelson Rockefeller's New York State Council for the Arts (NYSCA), and William Baumol and William Bowen's analysis of the economic prospects for the performing arts. Although these arts policy visionaries differed in their emphases, they all believed passionately in the centrality of the arts to an advanced civilization and shared a certain set of elite assumptions:

- The arts can be categorized into high and lesser art forms—that is, a strong distinction between "art" and "culture" can be made;
- The arts, especially the high arts, greatly benefit Americans as individuals and as a society;
- If support for the arts is left to the private market, not enough high art—and therefore not enough great art—will be created.

The NEA founders were also convinced that, "If we build it, they will come"; that is, they believed that average Americans would learn to love the high arts if only given the opportunity.[1]

But passage of the NEA's enabling legislation was by no means certain. Some opponents disliked the whole idea of public support for the arts, arguing, for example, that "poverty is good for the arts," that there are higher priorities for government,

[1] Author's interpretation based on readings from U.S. Congress (1961, 1962); Baumol and Bowen (1965, 1966); Netzer (1978); Larson (1983); Keller (1990); and Mark (1990). Zeigler (1994, p. 39) quotes Agnes deMille, one of the founding members of the National Council on the Arts, as saying: "Our intent from the beginning was to help the highest, the best."

and that public support would displace existing private support (Baumol and Bowen, 1966, pp. 371–2). Other opponents had no problem with public support in principle but were leery of creating a European-style "Ministry of Culture" centered in Washington, D.C. (U.S. Congress, 1961; U.S. Congress, 1962).[2] This was partly because they feared that a "Ministry of Culture" type of organization would discourage diversity of artistic expression. But they also feared that a centralized arts bureaucracy would widen existing cultural disparities between the big cities and smaller cities and rural areas.

To win over this second set of opponents, a key provision of the NEA's enabling legislation was that a partnership be established between the federal government and the states.[3] This partnership had three main goals:

- To ensure access to quality arts experiences for all Americans,
- To maintain a degree of local control over public funding of arts and culture, and
- To achieve broad-based political support for public funding of the arts.[4]

The first goal derived from a belief in state government's superior ability to find and nurture arts providers in smaller cities and rural areas. The second goal recognized the desire of local people to keep arts grantmaking from being dominated by people outside their states. The third goal sought to ensure that a broad spectrum of American voters would understand and appreciate how public spending on the arts was improving their communities and their lives.[5]

States wanting to receive federal arts money were required to form their own arts agencies and make financial commitments to them through legislative appropriations. There was no automatic pass-through; state legislators and the people they represented had to show their appreciation for federally funded programs by matching federal money. In most states, however, the ratio of the state-to-federal-dollar commitment remained considerably less than one-to-one for some time.[6] Not until 1974 did all 50 states even begin to appropriate funds of their own for the arts. In

---

[2] Some prominent artists and arts organizations—including, notably, the American Symphony Orchestra League—were among this group. See, for example, U.S. Congress, 1961, 1962; Netzer, 1978; and Zeigler, 1994.

[3] See, for example, U.S. Congress, 1961, and Larson, 1983, both of which make clear how little vision there was for a system of state-level support of the arts independent of the NEA.

[4] Author's interpretation based on readings from U.S. Congress, 1961, 1962; Scott, 1970; NEA, 1978; Larson, 1983; DiMaggio, 1991; Love, 1991; and SAA vision and mission statements.

[5] A short-term goal was to get political support for the NEA from members of Congress by setting aside money for their home states and districts. See, for example, Larson, 1983, p. 177.

[6] According to Scott (1970, p. 381), in FY 1967, just 11 states plus the District of Columbia and Puerto Rico received $50,000 in federal funds based on a 1:1 match. Twenty-eight states or jurisdictions received $25,000 in nonmatching federal planning grants plus slightly more than $12,000 in matching grants. The rest were "not yet prepared to raise matching funds" and thus received just the nonmatching $25,000 planning grants.

fact, the lure of federal money provided by the NEA was what motivated most states to establish their own arts agencies (Scott, 1970; Netzer, 1978; DiMaggio, 1991; Mulcahy, 2002).[7]

The NEA's catalytic role in the development of state-level support for the arts had somewhat paradoxical consequences. Although the federal-state partnership was created (in large part) to offset possible cultural domination by Washington, there was no positive vision of what the SAAs themselves should be. Many SAAs borrowed their enabling statutes from NYSCA, which itself had been one of the primary models for the NEA (NEA, 1978; Netzer, 1978). The result was that, like NYSCA and the NEA, most of the early SAAs operated under elite assumptions about the arts. Their missions, organization, and strategies were essentially all copied from NYSCA and the NEA.

A Supply-Side Approach

In the early years, a clear priority for almost all arts agencies—state and federal—was to build up the supply of the arts. Many states considered a supply-side approach necessary because, especially in rural areas, there was no "art" in which state residents could participate—at least, none recognized as such under the prevailing definitions.[8] Because Americans could not demand to have what they didn't know about, the strategy for increasing arts participation across America was to give grants to arts providers.

Following the precedent set by the NEA, SAAs' grantmaking process had three significant features:

- It severely limited the set of eligible grant applicants,
- It assigned arts activity to discipline-based categories, and
- It relied heavily on specialized expertise for determining which eligible providers within particular categories should be funded.

By limiting the set of eligible applicants to artists and nonprofit arts organizations, SAAs hoped to increase the number of people and organizations dedicated to making and presenting art—without duplicating existing commercial arts activities

[7] Six of the eight SAAs established prior to 1965 were voluntary organizations that received almost no state money. NYSCA and the Institute of Puerto Rican Arts and Culture were clear exceptions. See Netzer, 1978.

[8] Fully 90 percent of Montana's nonprofit arts organizations, for example, were incorporated after 1967, when the arts council was established. Nevertheless, we are conscious of the risk of overgeneralization: In a few states, the strategy was self-consciously "demand-side" from the beginning. In North Carolina, for example, the arts council's first steps were to build a network of local arts councils with the aim of increasing community-level demand for the arts. Aspects of this demand-side model for public support of the arts will be explored in future monographs.

and without allowing anyone to profit unduly from government largesse.[9] By many measures, they were tremendously successful: In FY 2000 alone, SAAs sponsored the work of over 2 million artists and almost 16,000 nonprofit arts organizations (NASAA, n.d.). Nevertheless, this policy led to many of the arts activities in which ordinary Americans participated being excluded from government grants—and often from governmental purview.

Categorization by discipline was a practical measure that allowed SAAs to compare similar types of organizations and activities when deciding grant awards. In the beginning, most SAAs adopted the grant program categories developed by the NEA. But disciplinary categorizations—and comparisons—became progressively harder to make as the list of art forms eligible for public support expanded. Discipline-specific programs also tended to create fiefdoms among program staff, hampering efforts to redistribute resources across programs.[10]

Finally, SAAs also borrowed the NEA's method for choosing grantees and setting the size of grant awards. With this method—peer panel review—grantees but not award sizes are largely determined according to the judgment of panelists "selected for their knowledge or expertise in the arts and their ability to interpret policies and review criteria" (Washington State Arts Commission, n.d.).[11] In the past, artistic merit served as the main criterion for selecting grantees, although arts organizations also had to demonstrate some degree of managerial competence. Grantees did not, however, generally have to demonstrate community interest in their work, or any sort of potential audience for it.

Elite Pillars of Support

In the early years, SAA grants primarily targeted big performing and presenting institutions (including museums) located in urban centers.[12] SAA grantees did include more touring projects and arts education programs than did NEA grantees, but both sets of grantees typically consisted of symphony orchestras, opera companies, ballet companies, and art museums (Arian, 1989; DiMaggio, 1991). One reason SAAs preferred to give grants to well-established institutions was that such institutions had the capacity to be accountable for public money. Another reason was that most state arts council members, as well as their advisory panelists, were affluent, highly educated and of white Western European origin (Harris, 1970; Pankratz, 1993). Many of these people

[9] Hansmann (1981) demonstrates why nonprofit organizations might be seen as more trustworthy vehicles for charitable donations—and, by extension, for public support—than for-profits are.

[10] Based on interviews. Also see Larson, 1983, and Marquis, 1995, on the experience of the NEA.

[11] Some states, as well as the NEA, now require at least one lay member (that is, someone who is not an arts professional) on each panel. Reflecting this change, panels are now often described as "advisory" rather "peer" panels.

[12] Clearly this was less true for states without major urban centers.

felt a deep responsibility to preserve and nurture the traditional European high arts, and they were both sincere and zealous about making their states places where the high arts could flourish. Benefits to the taxpaying public were considered as given.

Few SAAs gave grants to individual artists in the early years; according to Netzer (1978), just ten SAAs offered artist fellowships in 1974. This was partly because it was easier to reach the larger institutions than to reach individual artists, who often were not aware of their eligibility for grants and, when they were aware, didn't know how to go about writing grant applications. The larger arts organizations, by way of contrast, often had professional grantwriters on staff. Many SAAs also favored arts institutions for grants because the unpredictable nature and quality of individual artists' work makes such grants more risky politically.

SAAs' initial role as conduits for federal arts money—combined with their emphasis on major urban institutions and mostly high art forms—meant that most SAAs didn't enjoy strong grass-roots political support within their states. Certainly the majority of Americans, for whatever reasons, did not attend or otherwise participate in live performances of the symphony or ballet, or visit art museums (DiMaggio and Useem, 1978; Love and Klipple, 1995). But most Americans did not actively oppose public assistance for the arts, and SAA council members and their peers on the boards of major arts institutions were in and of themselves a potent political force (DiMaggio and Pettit, 1999; Kupcha, 1979; Arian, 1989). In many states, the leadership and friends of the major institutions agreed to lobby for their SAA's budget in return for a steady flow of grants.[13] They believed that, given the opportunity for education and exposure to the high arts, their fellow citizens would soon come to appreciate and agree with this arrangement.

For the first ten years or more, the arrangement seemed to work well for arts institutions and SAAs alike. State legislative appropriations for the arts (though still small relative to those for areas such as public health and education) more than tripled, and an increasing proportion of SAA program funds found their way to major high arts institutions (NASAA, 2000; Arian, 1989; DiMaggio, 1991). In fact, nonprofit arts organizations of all shapes and sizes seemed to prosper: Between 1968 and 1979, the number of nonprofit literary publishers, for example, grew by over 50 percent.[14] Participation in cultural events, as measured by audience size, also grew rapidly (Schwarz, 1983). The high arts moved out from their beachheads in cities such as New York, Chicago, and San Francisco, spreading rapidly across the country.

---

[13] For example Arian (1989, pp. 70–1) describes an arrangement involving the Pennsylvania Council on the Arts whereby "six major institutions in Philadelphia and Pittsburgh used their political influence in the legislature to help secure an increased appropriation for the agency in return for large, prearranged grants." Savage (1989) describes a similar sort of arrangement between the major Californian arts institutions and the California Arts Council. Again, this was less true for states lacking major urban centers.

[14] A lack of data for the early part of the decade makes it impossible to estimate accurately the growth of nonprofit arts organizations as a whole. See Schwartz, 1983.

CHAPTER THREE

The 1970s: Populist Cracks in the Pillar

Populist Criticisms of SAAs

By the mid-1970s, cracks in the political pillars supporting many SAAs had begun to appear. Critics argued that SAAs' political *quid pro quo* with the major arts institutions in their states had led to

- An inequitable distribution of funds across geographic areas and income levels (that is, too much money was going to major institutions), and
- Insufficient participation in or control over decision making at the local or community level (Arian, 1989; Eddy, 1970; Adams and Goldbard, 1995).

Essentially, these were the same concerns voiced by many opponents of the NEA at its founding, only now they were being expressed at the state level. But in light of the broad social and cultural changes sweeping through American society by the mid-1970s, more profoundly populist criticisms were also being heard.

The populist critics of the 1970s raised several new issues. First, they complained that SAAs (and the NEA) had ignored significant, even transcendent artistic endeavors originating from cultural communities outside the mainstream of American art. They argued, for example, that patterns of public funding had served to "perpetuate hierarchichal cultural patterns" by "pretending the high arts are acultural and universal, while the rest is anthropological and social" (Keller, 1990, p. 154). In other words, they believed that great art is produced by many, if not most, cultures around the world, including folk cultures indigenous to America.

Another complaint grew from the recognition that the fruits of America's investment in a geographically dispersed arts infrastructure were still being consumed by a very narrow segment of the population. By the late 1970s, the build-it-and-they-will-come philosophy was no longer widening the arts audience. Both federal and state agencies were continuing to help build the arts, but the participants were mostly from one class. In other words, nonprofit high arts producers had expanded dramatically in both numbers and resources, but growth in consumer demand for their programs had come primarily from highly educated elites (DiMaggio and Useem, 1978; Robinson, 1985; Kreidler, 1996; McCarthy et al., 2001).[1] According to the populist critics, the incipient demand for an "art of their own" that originated from the poor, the less well-educated and from cultural minorities had never been satisfied (Arian, 1989; Danto, 1999).

Finally, a third charge of the populist critics was that, in seeking to support only "the highest and the best" (from whatever cultural tradition), arts agencies were taking a far too limited view of the ways in which Americans can benefit from the arts. In addition to acknowledging the pleasure and prestige associated with high artistic achievement, they stressed the connection between cultural participation and such public benefits as increased creativity, greater tolerance of and respect for diversity, and higher levels of civic engagement (Adams and Goldbard, 1978). In other words, the promotion of "great art" was not the only rationale for public support of the arts.

SAA Responses to Populist Criticisms

Responses to populist criticisms of the arts agencies differed across states. Many SAAs made significant programmatic changes, such as introducing folk arts and "expansion arts" grant programs that targeted rural and minority ethnic communities.[2] Many also either introduced or directed more resources toward programs for community-based artists and for arts education.

California, for example, made sweeping changes to address the highly visible tension that had erupted between those holding elite and those holding populist views of the types of arts activities a public agency should support. In 1976, California Governor Jerry Brown completely restructured the arts commission that had been founded in 1963, replacing it with a counterculture council of artists that dramatically (and vocally) reduced support for major arts institutions. This new agency—the California Arts Council—emphasized local artists and community involvement, setting up resident arts programs for prisons, putting working artists in elementary schools, and funding legal aid groups for artists (Addison, 1976).

But the California Arts Council resisted ultimate community control: Plans to put council resources under the administrative direction of the counties were rejected because the Council was "wary of turning state funds over to county governments

[1] For example, DiMaggio and Useem (1978) looked at "virtually all major surveys of actual and potential arts consumers conducted in the United States since 1961" (p. 142). They concluded that "the ranks of those who attend museums and theater, opera, symphony and ballet performances are dominated by the wealthy and well-educated, most of whom are professionals and managers" (p. 156).

[2] The states followed the NEA in both these areas. For an account of the creation of the NEA's folk arts and expansion arts programs, see Zeigler, 1994.

that were often controlled by conservative politicians, particularly in the rural regions" (Savage, 1989, p. 453). One proponent of decentralization commented at the time, "Instead of arrogant patrons, we now have arrogant artists" in control (Addison, 1976, p. 318).[3]

Several other SAAs did decentralize, either by choice or because of legislative mandates, setting aside funds to be regranted through networks of local agencies. For example, in Minnesota, a few small but politically influential local arts councils complained that the Minnesota State Arts Council did not represent the interests of their constituents—and was passing on too great a share of state arts resources to the major high arts institutions in Minneapolis and St. Paul. In 1976, Minnesota legislators responded by changing the council's enabling legislation (and its name), and formally setting aside 27 percent of the new Minnesota State Arts Board's (MSAB's) budget to support a system of 11 local regional arts councils.[4] With MSAB acting as their fiscal agent, these 11 councils were responsible for assessing arts needs, developing programs and services to meet those needs, and distributing grants to fund local artists and smaller organizations within their local region.

As Figure 3.1 shows, the establishment of the local regional councils created essentially a two-tiered system of public support for Minnesota arts providers: The larger organizations were funded either by MSAB or by the NEA, and very small arts organizations were almost exclusively funded by the local regional councils.[5] As a result, even though small grass-roots organizations received their funding via the MSAB budget, their loyalties—and those of their communities—tended to be to the local regionals rather than to MSAB.

In 1979, legislators in Massachusetts went even further than those in Minnesota, bypassing the existing arts council—the Massachusetts Council on the Arts and Humanities (MCAH)—to create a second, entirely separate state agency dedicated to supporting the arts at the community level. This new agency, the Massachusetts Arts Lottery Council (MALC), distributed lottery revenues to arts councils in towns around the state using a formula that took into account each town's population and property values. MALC strived to balance out Massachusetts residents' cultural opportunities by giving less-affluent communities more weight in its distribution formula. As had hap-

---

[3] The California Arts Council did eventually decentralize, but not completely—and not until after many of its more radical grantmaking decisions had been excoriated in the media and by prominent members of the legislature and the public (Kupcha, 1979).

[4] I use the modifier *local regional,* to differentiate these Minnesotan councils, which consist of small groups of counties, from the seven (now six) interstate regional arts organizations that were also established by the NEA during the 1970s.

[5] The eligibility threshold for an MSAB Institutional Support Program (ISP) grant is now fairly low, reducing Minnesota's two-tiered nature of arts support, at least theoretically. In FY 2004, organizations eligible for an ISP grant could be as small as $128,000 in revenue. Further, very small organizations may be eligible for special project grants. See www.arts.state.mn.us/index.html.

Figure 3.1
Minnesota's System of Public Funding for the Arts After Decentralization

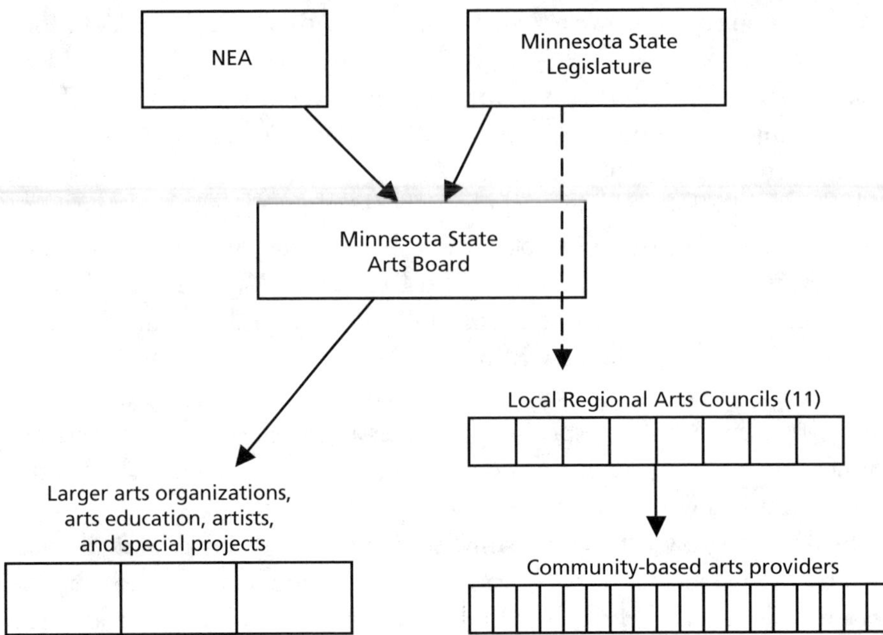

pened in Minnesota, one result was a two-tiered system of support for providers. According to the Massachusetts Cultural Council (MCC) (n.d., p. 5), "[T]he emergence of MALC had a significant impact in terms of increasing the geographic distribution of state moneys for the arts." But MCAH was cut off from its grassroots base even more firmly than MSAB had been in Minnesota.

By the end of the decade, nine SAAs were operating or in the process of establishing decentralization programs designed to make them more responsive to the diverse geographic and cultural communities within their states (NASAA, 1995).[6] Many more had pursued less-dramatic strategies to achieve populist goals, such as allocating more resources to arts education, folk arts and crafts, the art of cultural minorities, and community-based artists and artistic activities. All of these programs had the additional objective of building a broader political base of support for state arts funding.

But although most SAAs greatly expanded their definition of who or what constituted an "arts provider," no SAA tampered with its basic self-view as a grantmaker, and most retained their emphasis on increasing arts production rather than consumption. The political result was disappointing: On the whole, local arts councils received much of the credit for the regrants run through the budgets of decentralized agencies, and

[6] These states were, in order of their decentralization program's adoption, Maryland (1975), Minnesota (1976), North Carolina (1977), New Jersey (1978), New York (1978), Massachusetts (1979), Virginia (1979), California (1981), and Michigan (early 1980s).

community-based artists and arts organizations did not turn out to be effective lobbying forces for their SAAs.[7]

At the same time, many people who believed firmly that an arts agency's first duty was to preserve and nurture excellence had begun to lose faith in SAAs. Others that retained their faith were beginning to lose their political clout. Not coincidentally, this was happening at the same time as their favored institutions' dominance over the cultural landscape was eroding as new theaters, dance groups, classical music groups, performance venues, and art museums and galleries proliferated across America in the late 1970s and 1980s (NEA, 1993a–d; Association of Performing Arts Presenters, 1995).

[7] For example, staffers at one SAA told us that their state legislators love their local arts agency regrant program—and frequently confuse locally sponsored arts activities with those they sponsor. This confusion works sometimes for and sometimes against the SAA.

CHAPTER FOUR

The 1980s: A Widening of the Cracks

Breakdown of the Quid Pro Quo

The cracks in the traditional model of support for state funding of the arts widened to a fissure in the early 1980s. President Reagan failed in his 1981 attempt to eliminate the NEA, but the NEA's federal appropriation fell by almost 10 percent between FY 1981 and FY 1982 (NASAA, 2000)—its first-ever decline in nominal terms. The resulting drop in NEA basic state grants—in combination with a severe nationwide recession—put SAAs under significant budgetary pressure, even forcing several to cut their staffs by 30 to 50 percent.

When SAA managers looked for allies in the crunch, many found that their efforts to diversify their programming had combined with broad cultural and demographic changes occurring in their states to erode a major pillar of their political support. Much of the leadership (and audience) of the major arts institutions was either unwilling or unable to undertake significant lobbying efforts for their SAAs (Urice, 1992). In other words, the quiet political *quid pro quo* between many SAAs and their major state art institutions had broken down. This was evidenced by the fact that arts institutions in many states began lobbying for their own line items rather than working for increases to their SAAs' overall budgets.[1] Between 1980 and 1990, the number of SAAs with legislative line items rose from 11 to 21 while line items as a share of total legislative appropriations grew from 2.8 to 12.8 percent (NASAA, 2000).[2]

One factor contributing to the breakdown was a change in the system for evaluating grant applications. During the 1960s and 1970s, most SAA grant review panel meetings were closed to the public, and little effort was made to exclude panelists with

[1] As described by NASAA (2003, p. 8), "Line items pass through an agency's budget directly to another entity. State and jurisdictional legislatures earmark recipients and amounts, while the SAA usually holds little or no influence over how the recipient will ultimately use the money."

[2] According to NASAA (2000), the number of states with legislative line items exceeding 10 percent of their legislative appropriation rose from 5 in 1980 to 12 in 1990.

conflicts of interest. In some cases, SAA staff or board members themselves played favorites. For example, for many years the executive committee of the Ohio Arts Council Board privately determined the amount (although not the beneficiaries) of each grant award. As a result, its distribution of grants was systematically uneven: Two major orchestras always received the maximum grant of $50,000, while a major art museum with an even larger operating budget received only $20,000. This practice ended with the 1975 enactment of Ohio's "Sunshine Law," which required open access to most governmental decision-making meetings. The Ohio Arts Council became one of the first SAAs to move to an open-door, no-conflict-of-interest grant review policy. By the end of the 1980s, most SAAs had followed Ohio's lead.[3]

With the breakdown of the *quid pro quo*, many SAAs looked for support from the statewide citizen arts advocacy groups that, not coincidentally, sprang up around the country in the late 1970s and early 1980s.[4] Between 1980 and 1990, at least 14 new statewide arts advocacy groups were born (Dworkin, 1991). Kentucky Citizens for the Arts provides a typical example: In 1981, at the instigation of the acting chairman of the (then) Kentucky Arts Commission, this advocacy group was formally launched in response to threatened cuts to the Commission's budget (Wooden, 2001). In Arizona and Idaho, the story was similar: Arizonans for Cultural Development was founded in 1981 by the directors of Arizona's major arts organizations; Arts for Idaho was founded in 1987 by the volunteer chairman of the arts commission. Both were created in an effort to boost state legislative appropriations for their SAAs (Dworkin, 1991).

SAAs generally encouraged the creation of statewide arts advocacy groups but soon recognized that they did not always share these groups' priorities. Regardless of why these groups had originally been founded, many of them came to be dominated—if not controlled outright—by major arts organizations that fiercely resisted SAA attempts to shift funds in other directions. Nevertheless, the majors perceived certain advantages to building coalitions with smaller organizations and rural art interests. In Minnesota, for example, Minnesota Citizens for the Arts (founded by the major Minneapolis-St. Paul area arts institutions) chose to put together an urban-rural coalition "[b]ecause more than half of the state was rural and many legislators were unresponsive to the concerns of urban arts organizations" (Dworkin, 1991, p. 207). Such coalitions, however, often proved unstable.

Straddling the Gap

With the economic recovery and consequent restoration of state budgets in the mid-1980s, SAAs were once again able to straddle the ideological gap between the populist

[3] Based on interviews.

[4] The first statewide arts advocacy group was the New York Concerned Citizens for the Arts, established in 1970 (Dworkin, 1991).

vision of funding diverse artistic expression and the elite vision of giving grants to encourage artistic excellence. Most SAAs, realizing that total reliance on the majors for political support was no longer a viable strategy, worked hard at reaching out to the increasingly culturally diverse populations within their states.[5] Their approach still focused on the supply side, however: Grant programs proliferated as SAAs attempted to get representation from ever smaller cultural subsegments of their state populations (Urice, 1992). At the same time, their dedication to preserving and nurturing excellence did not diminish. SAAs' general operating support contributed only a small amount to the bottom line for most large established institutions, but that support continued to represent between 40 and 60 percent of most SAAs' grantmaking budgets (Arian, 1989; DiMaggio, 1991).

In sum, although the early 1980s were a grim time for many SAAs, most had managed to regain lost ground by the end of the decade. Strong state budgets and a booming economy meant lots of grant money to give out and a financially healthier arts sector to receive it. Nevertheless, some observers believed that the SAAs had simply dodged a bullet (Urice, 1992). They had managed to expand their constituent bases, but their strongest advocates still consisted primarily, if not exclusively, of actual and potential grantees. These arts-provider advocates were committed and (sometimes) well organized, but it was hard for them to convince state legislators that their support for public spending on the arts was representative of the citizenry at large.[6] By the end of the 1980s, SAAs had at least two main political tasks to accomplish: Convince average citizens that the arts are important to their lives, and convince them that their SAA is important to the arts.

---

[5] This desire to reach out beyond their traditional grantee base was not just a response to a political imperative. It was also a recognition of the exciting, highly pluralistic nature of the arts activities taking place around them.

[6] Opinions on the effectiveness of state arts advocacy efforts vary widely. According to Marquis (1995), for example, the state arts lobby in the 1970s "was so well organized that governors found it lethal to cut entitlements" (p. 140). However, many within the arts community complain of their lack of influence over public spending on the arts.

CHAPTER FIVE

The 1990s to the Present: A Watershed for SAAs?

The 1990s can be seen as a watershed for SAAs in several respects. Debates over what artists should or should not do with public money created an even higher level of political turmoil than had rocked state agencies in the 1970s. In the early 1990s (and again in the early 2000s), SAAs also suffered as a result of state fiscal crises. They had faced such crises in earlier years, but these were deeper than any they had collectively seen before. And the 1990s brought something new: The American public, increasingly distrustful of government programs in general, was involving itself more and more in the debate over public funding of the arts. Together, these trends led to calls for greater public accountability by SAAs.

Budgetary Woes and Political Turmoil

Less than ten years after President Reagan's attempt to eliminate the NEA, SAAs' inability to articulate and implement a vision for making themselves (if not the arts) indispensable to a broad spectrum of their states' citizens became clear. In the early 1990s, public arts funders found themselves once again under attack. This time, their opponents achieved a significant success. Intense pressure to balance the federal budget and public outrage at what were perceived to be artistic excesses led to an almost 40 percent cut in the NEA's FY 1996 budget—resources that, as of fall 2003, have not been fully restored.[1] And although the primary target of the budget slashers was the NEA and not the SAAs (the budget share allocated to the states under the NEA's basic

[1] According to one reviewer, "[I]t was conservative politicians' outrage more than public outrage" at perceived artistic excesses. My own informal (and entirely unscientific) surveys suggest, however, that the outrage extended to many self-designated political liberals.

state grant program was actually increased as a result of the crisis), SAAs did not remain immune.[2]

In purely budgetary terms, the net effect of the NEA cut on SAAs was severe, at least initially, because the increase in the pass-through to SAAs was not enough to offset the very large reduction in the NEA's budget. Further, the cut in federal funds was exacerbated by concurrent cuts in state legislative appropriations. In FY 1992, a particularly bad year, nine states experienced cuts of more than 20 percent in their legislative appropriations (excluding line items), and, as shown in Table 5.1, five states faced cuts of more than 35 percent.[3]

Table 5.1
States with Biggest Cuts in Legislative Appropriations, FY 1992

State	Percent Decline
Tennessee	64.6
Massachusetts	64.2
Virginia	62.6
New York	38.7
Michigan	37.0

SOURCE: NASAA, 2000.
NOTE: Not including line items.

In fact, 1989–93 saw sharp declines in state legislative appropriations across the board (Figure 5.1), declines that, in contrast to those of previous years, affected SAAs around the country rather than those of only a a few key states (Love, 1991).[4] The period 1994–98 then put appropriations growth back in positive territory, but at a much slower pace than before. For the decade as a whole, total legislative appropriations fell by an inflation-adjusted 1.5 percent (1989–98), after having increased 8.8 percent in the previous decade. And, as mentioned above, this was on top of sharp declines in basic state grants from the NEA in 1994–98 (Figure 5.2).

Cuts in state legislative appropriations for the arts were the result, in large part, of the nationwide recession that hit in the early 1990s. But the way these cuts played out in many states revealed the weakness of local political support for SAAs. In Massachusetts, for example, MCAH (established in 1967) and MALC (established in 1979) were forced to merge amid continuing charges of funding elitism. In 1992, the budget of the new, combined council, the MCC, was lower than the sum of the two original

[2] In 1973, Congress set the NEA pass-through of program funds to the states at 20 percent. In 1990, Congress voted to increase the pass-through to 27.5 percent, with an additional 7.5 percent reserved for competitive grants in support of rural and inner-city programs. The proportion dedicated to the states was raised again in 1996, to 40 percent. DiMaggio (1991) discusses the possible programmatic impacts of the devolution of arts funding from the federal to the state and local levels.

[3] Note, however, that state legislative appropriations can vary tremendously from year to year. The Tennessee Arts Commission, for example, experienced a 23 percent cut in FY 1990, a 3.5 percent increase in FY 1991, a 64.6 percent cut in FY 1992, and a 71.6 percent increase in FY 1993.

[4] Expressed in 1982–84 constant dollars as measured by the Bureau of Labor Statistics' Consumer Price Index (CPI).

Figure 5.1
Percent Change in SAA Legislative Appropriations, FY 1969–2003 (1982–84 constant dollars)

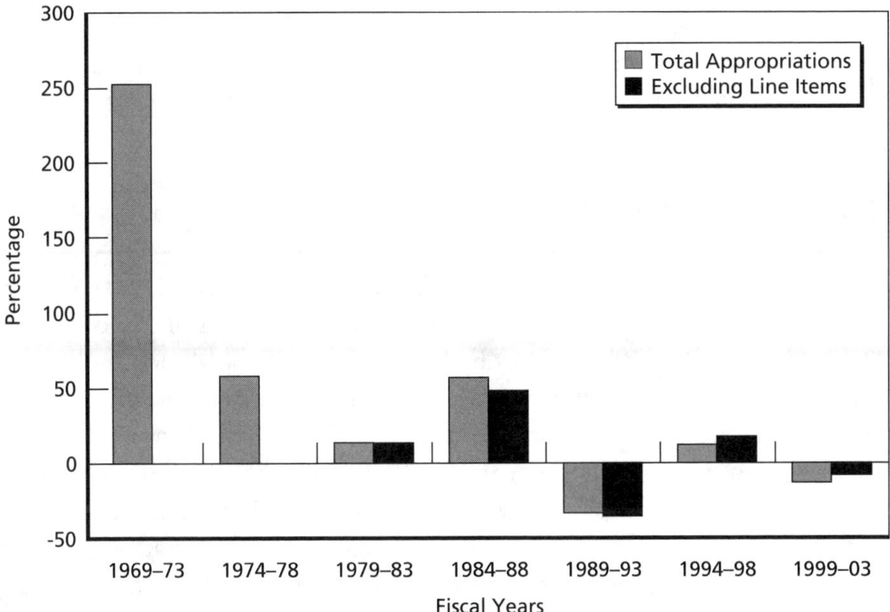

SOURCE: NASAA, 2000; U.S. Bureau of Labor Statistics.

Figure 5.2
Percent Change in NEA Basic State Grants, FY 1969–2003

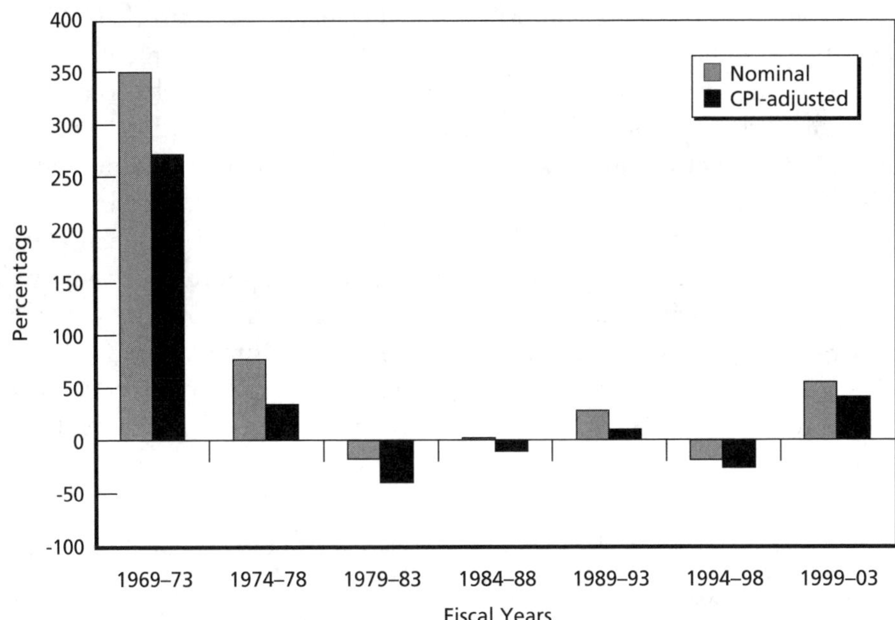

SOURCE: NASAA, 2000; U.S. Bureau of Labor Statistics.
NOTE: Data do not include grants awarded to states under competitive NEA programs. Basic State Grants were replaced by the Basic State Plan component of the NEA's Partnership Agreement with states in 1997.

agencies had been in 1981 (MCC, n.d.). In Montana, the arts council was forced into a bitter struggle against a well-organized faction of religious conservatives that came close to shutting the council down in 1997. Perhaps most damaging of all, many SAAs found their budget woes were met with indifference. Willing enough to see SAA budgets grow during good economic times, voters—or, at least, their elected representatives—made little effort to keep them from collapsing when times got bad.

A Different Sort of Crisis?

Were the 1990s really much different for SAAs than previous periods of budgetary woe and political turmoil had been? In some ways not: By the end of the decade, public outrage over perceived artistic excesses had faded from the headlines, and most SAAs once again saw their state legislative appropriations increase. But the events of the 1990s forced many SAA managers to consider more radical solutions to their agencies' weak position within state government. Well before the budgetary meltdown of the early 2000s, they were exploring ways to transform their agencies so as to raise the profile of the arts—and their agencies—with the citizens of their states. They now also realized that any such transformation would have to account for two new realities of American cultural and political life.

First, the 1990s saw perhaps the culmination of a major shift in American social attitudes that had become evident in the 1970s. Just as curriculum reform had profoundly challenged the world of education, challenges to the accepted canon of great art had become mainstream (Conforti, 1989; Levine, 1996; Larson, 1997; Campbell, 1998). Jazz and other entire genres had finally been fully accepted into the high arts pantheon.[5] Answers to the question, What is culture versus what is art?, though still forcefully disputed, had become very much slanted toward inclusiveness.[6]

For SAAs, one of the implications of this shift was that the dominance of the "great art" rationale for public support of the arts—and the relative importance of the major high arts institutions in American society and politics—had clearly diminished. It wasn't (necessarily) that there were fewer supporters of these types of institutions or that their supporters were any less passionate. But the supporters of other types of art and art experiences had achieved legitimacy—and had become politicized. The political *quid pro quo* that had worked (albeit with decreasing effectiveness) for many SAAs and their major arts institutions from the 1970s on was simply no longer tenable.[7]

---

[5] For example, it was not until 1996 that a jazz ensemble—the Lincoln Center Jazz Orchestra—became a full constituent of the Lincoln Center for the Performing Arts. The first-ever education, performance, and broadcast facility devoted to jazz—Frederick P. Rose Hall—is slated to open at Lincoln Center in fall 2004 (Jaggi, 2003; Jazz at Lincoln Center, n.d.).

[6] For arguments against a more inclusive view of the arts, see, for example, Brustein, 1997, 2000.

The second feature that made the 1990s a watershed for SAAs was a shift in American attitudes toward the overall roles and responsibilities of government. From education to welfare to criminal justice—even in the area of national defense—voters were demanding that public-sector institutions become

- More responsive to the public's interests and
- More able to demonstrate the results of their efforts to the public (Osborne and Gaebler, 1993; Kettl, 1998).

The idea of a government that works better and costs less resonated at all levels, but perhaps especially at the state level, where recession-induced revenue declines often hit up against balanced budget requirements. With so many state government programs making claims on a limited purse, any government activities that large segments of the population deemed "nonessential"—such as support for the arts—were highly vulnerable.

Cash Machines Without Clout

In fact, during the 1990s, many SAAs were forced to grapple with the problem of near-irrelevancy to the political establishments of their states.[8] General operating support grants were often spread so thin that they became peripheral to the finances of the institutions they were intended to aid.[9] And while many artists and smaller arts groups and organizations still valued SAA money, and the SAA imprimatur, these types of grantees had not generally formed effective political coalitions. The supply-side strategy of supporting arts producers had successfully turned many SAAs into cash machines, but without much clout—and often without much money.

As for Americans in general, and even artists themselves, many seem not to know their state *has* an arts agency. The New Jersey State Council on the Arts (NJSCA) found this out in a series of focus groups and roundtables conducted in 1996 as part of its strategic planning process. When NJSCA staff spoke to artists around the state they found that:

---

[7] Kammen (1996) argues that the end of the cold war in 1989 also had a profound effect on public support for government funding of culture, as "many of those who had long feared alien ideologies subsequently projected their anxieties onto domestic 'enemies' such as artists [and] intellectuals" (p. 135).

[8] For example, staff members at one START agency told us that their agency was "the province of the first lady"—and "not even on the governor's radar screen." Clearly this perception varies by state and by governor, but it appears to be quite widely held.

[9] California offers perhaps the most extreme example. In FY 2001, the California Arts Council gave the San Francisco Ballet Association a $135,558 organizational support grant. This came to less than one-half of one percent of the San Francisco Ballet's FY 2000 net income of over $27 million. (The San Francisco Ballet also received an $18,000 Exemplary Arts Education program grant in FY 2001, but presumably it was closely tied to particular educational activities.) Author's calculation based on data from the Guide Star Database of Nonprofit Organizations (www.guidestar.org).

1. "Most New Jersey artists didn't know who we were"; and
2. Those that did, "didn't like us!"[10]

Managers at NJSCA attribute the latter response to the fact that the agency had been sending out approximately 15 times as many letters rejecting artists' grant applications as awarding grants. But the fact that most of the artists had not even heard of the council was disturbing. If *artists* are unaware of the services NJSCA provides, managers worried, what does that imply about the ordinary, "non-arts" citizen?

Ohio Arts Council staff had a similar disheartening experience when they surveyed nearly 8,000 people and organizations throughout Ohio in 1998–99. They found that, "while three out of four Ohioans believe state tax dollars should be used to support the arts, only 28 percent of those same respondents know that state tax dollars *are currently used* to support the arts in Ohio" (Ohio Arts Council, 2001, p. 9). As in New Jersey, many of the people across the state did not know the arts council existed.

This lack of external visibility doesn't necessarily mean that SAAs are doing a bad job: State residents may well be unaware of the many departments, agencies, councils, and commissions operated under the authority of their state government. But maintaining an almost invisible profile is not a recipe for growth for most political organizations. SAAs' lack of visibility suggests that most people perceive them as, at best, peripheral to their needs—and therefore expendable.

Many SAA managers became convinced in the 1990s that, if SAAs were to thrive rather than merely survive from year to year, they would have to undergo profound philosophical changes in their orientation.[11] They recognized the changes they sought had to help their agencies to:

- Find common ground in a pluralistic, multicultural America, where opinions about what sort of art should be publicly funded are divided;
- Respond to taxpayers' desire for an efficient and effective government; and
- Demonstrate the value of what they do to a majority of Americans, including those who are largely indifferent to art.

In both New Jersey and Ohio, for example, SAA managers responded to their survey findings by greatly expanding their outreach to state residents.

However, many SAA managers were unsure how to go about making changes. Moreover, they did not have the time or resources necessary for pursuing change strategies in any systematic way.

---

[10] Reported by NJSCA managers. Quoted by permission.

[11] SAAs were not the only state-level public-sector organizations to feel battered and bruised as a result of the budget battles of the 1990s. Many public higher education institutions also suffered a crisis of confidence and sought to put themselves on a firmer footing with the public. See, for example, Joseph C. Burke and Associates, 2002, and Callan, 2002.

CHAPTER SIX

Looking to the Future: The START Initiative

What will it take for SAAs to become less marginalized, both with respect to their state political establishments and with respect to the rich variety of arts activities taking place around their states? One strategy that SAAs have identified as key is to encourage a wider spectrum of the American public to become involved in the arts. In fact, cultural participation, and ways to promote it, was the theme of the first-ever joint annual meeting of NASAA and Americans for the Arts in July 2001, and will be again for the second joint meeting in 2004.[1]

SAAs' heightened interest in promoting greater cultural participation has coincided with a series of Wallace Foundation initiatives targeting the same goal. Since the early to mid-1990s, Wallace has been investing in—and drawing lessons from—arts and cultural organizations that consider community involvement to be as central to their missions as artistic excellence is. Wallace's desire to leverage what it has learned about participation building, in addition to leveraging its monetary resources, led it to conclude that SAAs would be valuable partners in its outreach efforts. Wallace's belief was (and is) that SAAs, as both leaders within their state arts communities and significant funders of the arts, have the potential to influence the programs and practices of American arts organizations in ways that a foundation alone cannot.

Evolution of the START Program

In 2000, Wallace sent out a request for proposals to all 56 SAAs, asking them to submit new or improved ideas for increasing cultural participation in their states or jurisdictions. This was the START initiative. Wallace expected successful applicants to try innovative approaches tailored to their individual environments. It also hoped to extract

[1] Americans for the Arts was created in 1996 as a result of the merger between the National Assembly of Local Arts Agencies and the American Council for the Arts, a nationwide arts advocacy organization.

from the START agency experiences "lessons learned" that would help other SAAs establish new standards and practices for building local arts participation.

In April 2001, it was announced that 13 SAAs had been selected to receive multiyear grants of between $500,000 and $1.1 million. By many measures, the successful proposals were quite innovative. Several START agencies proposed to teach themselves the latest audience-development and other participation-building techniques so that they in turn could pass them on to selected local arts organizations. Several also proposed to create new grant categories for demonstration projects to model these techniques. Relatively few of the proposals, however, looked beyond traditional nonprofit arts providers as their instruments for boosting participation.[2]

Initial distribution of the grant money began in mid-2001, and most of the agencies were well into their planning phases by early 2002.[3] By this time, however, state economies around the country had begun to weaken dramatically. Just six months later, many states were in full-blown recession and the SAA budget cutting had begun.

As the various state budget crises began to unfold, both the START agencies and Wallace realized that political and budgetary concerns were siphoning time and energy from the agencies' formal START programs. Wallace decided to enlist the help of Mark H. Moore, a professor at Harvard's Kennedy School of Government who has spent much of his career developing concepts and tools for public sector strategic management.[4] The START agency managers who attended Moore's first session, in July 2002, were galvanized by what they heard and discussed: The conceptual framework he provided not only immediately helped them to make sense of their situation, it also gave them much-needed insights on possible future strategic directions.

Because Moore's ideas were so well received, Wallace put together a series of workshops, telephone conferences, individual site visits, and suggested readings, many of which feature Moore and all of which are ongoing as of fall 2003. The idea is to explore the roles and responsibilities of SAAs as public sector agencies—and then to determine what those roles and responsibilities mean for each agency's approach to building cul-

---

[2] Two agencies that did look beyond traditional providers from the beginning were the Ohio Arts Council and the Washington State Arts Commission. Ohio proposed (among other things) to explore the role of faith-based institutions as venues for arts experiences; Washington focused on nontraditional providers in minority cultural communities.

[3] The proposals were reviewed by Wallace staff as well as a national advisory panel drawn from the arts community. According to Wallace, the agencies selected to receive START grants demonstrated the following characteristics:

1. "an active and sustained history (usually of ten years or more) of building public participation in the arts through high-quality artistic programs of national distinction;
2. a mission consistent with and supportive of the goals of START;
3. a record of developing and/or presenting high-quality and effective public programs;
4. competence in planning, program development, public engagement and marketing;
5. stability of finances, governance, and staff." (Quoted from a personal letter to the author from The Wallace Foundation.)

[4] Moore's 1995 book, *Creating Public Value*, lays out many of his ideas. Key ideas contained in his work, as applied to SAAs, will be discussed at greater length in a future monograph.

tural participation. The various START participation-building programs are continuing but on a somewhat secondary track: For now, the primary focus of the START program is the START agencies themselves.

Public Agencies: Public Servants

What is it about Moore's message that so excited the START agency managers? The crux of it is that, as public agencies, their ultimate constituency comprises all residents of their states. This in itself is not new; SAA mission statements reveal that most SAAs already believe that serving their state citizens is at the front and center of their activities.[5] In practice, however, SAAs often seem to equate service to the arts aficionados, artists, and nonprofit arts organizations that make up their state arts community with service to the general public. They have worked hard to meet the needs and interests of arts providers ("the field") but have not always ensured that the arts providers have, in turn, met the needs and interests of the broader public.

Perhaps the clearest proof of this failure to attend to the broader public comes from SAA grant program allocations. Evidence from the 13 START agencies suggests that program assessments are based on whether programs "meet the needs of the field," not the needs of the various communities around their states. More than one agency told us its most-used indicator for deciding whether to retain a program is the number of applications it receives. This is so even though all SAAs embark on periodic strategic planning processes that, in theory, should provide them with public input for their decision making.

As a result—and especially prior to the 1990s—some SAAs' relative budget shares across broad program categories have remained static for years. New programs have been added as SAAs identified new provider constituencies, but old programs have lingered.[6] Within programs, the tendency has been to fund the same institutions over and over, especially in the case of general operating support. As the executive director of one START agency put it, "[o]nce an organization gets on [general operating sup-

---

[5] For example, four SAA mission statements chosen at random included the following:

Delaware: "dedicated to nurturing and supporting the arts to enhance the quality of life for all Delawareans";

New Jersey: "to improve the quality of life of this state, its people and communities by helping the arts to flourish";

North Dakota: "to ensure that the role of the arts in the life of our communities will continue to grow and will play a significant part in the welfare and educational growth of our citizens";

Washington: "to cultivate a thriving environment for creative expression and appreciation for the arts for the benefit of all."

[6] This was particularly true prior to the 1990s. During the 1990s, however, several states made significant programmatic changes. Programs funded externally (for example, by private foundations) rather than by legislative appropriations were eliminated when the external funding source dried up. Programs were also "merged" or "transformed."

port], it's almost impossible to get them off unless they do something that's outright fraudulent!"

For some START agencies, therefore, the idea of eliminating entitlements in order to create new programs and services that benefit a broader public is extremely welcome. They are eager to develop all sorts of partnerships—be they with other government agencies, non-arts civic institutions, local communities, for-profit and amateur arts groups, etc.—any person, group, or institution with the potential to get more and different kinds of people involved in the arts is a candidate. However, even these START agencies are quite anxious about diverting scarce resources away from artists and arts groups they have long known and respected. They still see themselves primarily as advocates for arts providers. The first response of most START agencies to Moore's message has thus been to revise their guidelines for existing grant programs. Their intent is to encourage grantees to be more attentive to community needs and interests.

Yet even these rather small steps can be difficult, as an anecdote related by a START agency staffer illustrates: A jazz presenter, recounting his dire financial situation, was pleading for money from the agency. The staffer, who has been very involved with the START initiative, responded, "We don't give you money because you need it." Startled, the jazz presenter replied, "You don't?" "No," said the staffer. "We give you money because you deliver something specific to the public that the state would like to have happen." According to the staffer, at some level her agency understood this prior to START, but lacked both the framework and the language for making it clear. Now they are in the midst of figuring out what that "something specific" looks like—in order to explain it to their would-be grantees. Most of the START agencies are doing likewise.

In any case, whether welcome or not, the kinds of changes implied by Moore's work do raise some difficult issues for SAAs. The sections that follow identify a few of these issues and briefly describe how some START agencies have begun to deal with them.

Where to Start with START: Strengthening Political Ties

On the surface, the idea of serving citizens rather than the arts community certainly sounds politically attractive. But the arts community is still the major source of political support for SAAs. Most SAA managers are understandably reluctant to risk alienating known backers in the hopes of gaining support from what is for now a largely passive and indifferent public. Further, state legislators themselves benefit politically from the grants provided to artists and arts organizations within their districts. Some legislators might well oppose new SAA policies that could jeopardize these grant allocations, for much the same reasons as SAAs themselves oppose them. Thus, while SAAs may find the move to a "citizens as customers" model politically desirable—and necessary—in the long run, the transition poses significant difficulties in the short run.

It makes sense, then, that each of the 13 START agency managers has assigned first priority to strengthening his or her relationships with elected state officials. This might have happened anyway, absent the START initiative, because of SAAs' sense of vulnerability following the 2002–04 budgets cuts. But stronger political ties make particular sense in the START context because of the challenges SAAs face in transitioning to a more citizen-focused mission. The START agency managers want to make sure they have solid political support if and when they decide to make substantive programmatic or other changes.

Therefore, Moore's work has so far had its biggest practical impact in the political arena. The Montana Arts Council, for example, set up a "listening tour" of one-on-one meetings with key legislators, the idea being not to ask them for money, but rather to get to know them personally in order to establish a connection between what they value and the arts. In New Jersey, NJSCA initiated a series of monthly e-mails to all 120 members of the state legislature. These "e-flashes" report on district-level activities that NJSCA programs and services have made possible. The Massachusetts Cultural Council convened a statewide arts leadership conference with a roundtable discussion featuring the Speaker of the House, the editor of *The Boston Globe*, the director of Boston's Museum of Fine Arts, and a senior manager at Fleet Bank. Other START agencies report similar efforts. For many of them, these efforts represent a significant change from just two years ago, when their approach to elected officials was often to "keep our heads low and hope we don't show up on their radar screen."[7]

Measuring SAA Performance

The START agencies are also beginning to reconsider how they define and measure their own performance. State law or administrative regulation requires most state agencies, including arts agencies, to produce "quantifiable data that provides meaningful information about program outcomes" (Willoughby and Melkers, 1998, p. 1). In the arts, this requirement has usually translated to such indicators as total funds requested by grant applicants, total number of grants, individuals served by SAA grant programs, and program expenditures as a percentage of total expenditures (NASAA, 1996). These types of indicators are useful for some purposes, but they essentially measure outputs and efficiency, not outcomes. That is, they quantify the number, types, and cost-effectiveness of SAA products and services, but not their impact on state residents.

As NASAA and the SAAs have long realized, measuring the effects of the arts—and of the arts agencies—on people and communities is inherently quite difficult. In fields such as public health, government spending can be directly and measurably linked to declines in infectious disease. But links between government spending, the vitality and diversity of local cultural environments, and other measures of community well-being are indirect and mostly unproven. Nevertheless, Moore has encouraged the

---

[7] Variations on this comment were made to the author during several of the 2002 site visits.

START agencies to put considerable time and thought into devising ways to demonstrate the value of what they do to state residents.

One reason is political: As shown by the recent budget cuts, many SAAs are finding it hard to make their case for public resources.[8] Better measures of outcomes could help SAA managers justify their programs to their state legislatures. But a more profound reason is that the search for ways to show their value could deepen SAAs' own understanding of their missions and help them identify where they can have the greatest impact. In searching for measures of what they want to achieve, SAAs must necessarily think harder about what it is they want to achieve. Whether it can ever really be quantified is another question.

Going to Where the People Are

Recognizing that only a small proportion of Americans regularly pass through the doors of traditional nonprofit arts institutions (Robinson et al., 1985; Robinson, 1993; Schuster, 1991), many SAAs have decided that they must "go to where the people are" in order to serve them better. Several have conducted statewide surveys to find out why, where, and how their citizens choose to participate in the arts. Often working with nontraditional partners—including some in state government—they are exploring ways to deepen and expand the cultural experiences of Americans who aren't comfortable or aren't interested in traditional nonprofit arts venues.

For example, after the Ohio Arts Council found that churches are the top gathering places for many Ohio communities, Council staff concluded that churches could become important venues for all sorts of arts and cultural events.[9] The Ohio Arts Council's Faith-Based Institution Performing Arts Touring Program, which brings international performing groups to churches and synagogues, was created to offer more Ohioans the opportunity to experience the art of other cultures in a setting where they feel comfortable.[10] According to an evaluation of the 2001 tour, attendance at tour events was close to capacity, and holding the events at faith-based institutions influenced the decision to attend for nearly 50 percent of attendees (Mattern and Kratz, 2002).

Nevertheless, the budgets of most, if not all, SAAs are tiny compared to the nonprofit arts sector they serve, and they are even tinier compared to all of the for-profit and avocational arts activities in their states. As grantmakers, SAAs' ability to support larger nonprofit organizations is already limited, and many, many small- to medium-

---

[8] Moore has emphasized, however, that given the unprecedented state fiscal crises of the early 2000s, there may have been little that some SAAs could do to protect their budgets.

[9] See the Council's *State of the Arts Report* (Ohio Arts Council, 2001), which was partly funded through the START initiative.

[10] As described in Starker, 2001, the program adheres to a strict separation of church and state: Religious programming is never presented, events are open to the public, and the host institutions receive no money. The program was renamed the International Music Performing Arts and Communities Tour (IMPACT) in 2003.

sized arts nonprofits get no state money at all. How, then, can SAAs extend their reach past the nonprofit arts world to the for-profit and avocational arts worlds and beyond? Can SAAs expect to have an impact in these areas?

Letting the People Decide

Finally, there is a philosophical, even ideological reason why serving arts providers may really be the best way to serve citizens: The general public may lack the knowledge and sophistication needed to make good choices about the arts. This was certainly the assumption of the NEA founders, who held to the top-down doctrine of "If we build it, they will come." Arguably, the situation has worsened in the past 20 years as the level of arts education has declined nationwide. Further, given that there currently is no consensus within the arts community itself on how public resources for the arts should be spent, it is not at all clear that allowing the general public a greater voice in decision making will help build consensus.

At present, all 56 SAAs have strategic planning processes that, in theory, are designed to identify and assess community needs and desires. Bus tours, telephone and mail surveys, focus groups, and "town meetings" all could be useful approaches for finding out what the public most wants from its SAAs. So far, however, the SAAs mostly seem to have connected with people already heavily involved in the arts.[11] In one state we visited, agency staff told us they had not opened up their strategic planning process to the general public because "[our statewide advocacy group] won't want to hear what people have to say."

And who is to say that this advocacy group is entirely wrong? With little exposure to the arts, the average American may not be able to make informed decisions about the allocation of public arts money. As noted by Izumi (1999, p. 17), "[I]f differing cultural products are to be appreciated, then education that teaches such appreciation is critical." But what is the best way to teach children or adults to critically appreciate the arts? And are SAAs in the best position to take on this challenge?

Conclusion

This short history of SAAs' evolution suggests that they are in search of a new mandate. Their original missions, roles, and structures are not suited to the cultural and political realities of American society at the beginning of the 21st century. When SAAs were founded, the arts were narrowly defined and states had very few nonprofit arts institutions. Today, the arts are broadly defined and nonprofit arts providers have become so numerous that SAAs can contribute modestly to only a tiny fraction of them. Both the

---

[11] To some extent, this may be unavoidable because those with the biggest stake in an area tend to be the most eager to have input into that area's decision making.

turbulence caused by this transition and the opportune funding that Wallace provided to 13 SAAs are stimulating all SAAs to rethink certain issues: the public purposes of the arts, how to promote people and communities through them, and how to identify what success would look like if it happened.

This study will provide future monographs on the progress of SAAs. It may turn out that they become pioneers in redefining government's proper role in supporting the arts in a pluralistic democracy. If that proves to be the case, we will all benefit from their efforts.

APPENDIX A

Summary Information for the 13 START Agencies, FY 2001

Agency	Per Capita Spending (Rank)[a]	Total Revenue[b]	START Grant
Arizona Commission on the Arts (ACA) Executive Director: Shelley Cohn 417 West Roosevelt Street Phoenix, AZ 85003	$0.76 (34)	$4.8 million	$500,000 over 5 years
California Arts Council (CAC) Executive Director: Barry Hessenius 1300 I Street, Suite 930 Sacramento, CA 95814	$2.01 (16)	$68.9 million	$600,000 over 3 years
Connecticut Commission on the Arts (CCA) Executive Director: Douglas Evans One Financial Plaza, 755 Main Street Hartford, CT 06103	$3.99 (3)	$21.1 million	$500,000 over 3.5 years
Kentucky Arts Council (KAC) Executive Director: Gerri Combs Old Capitol Annex 300 West Broadway Frankfort, KY 40601–1980	$1.01 (30)	$4.7 million	$500,000 over 3 years
Massachusetts Cultural Council (MCC) Executive Director: Mary Kelley 10 St. James Street, 3rd Floor Boston, MA 02116	$2.80 (8)	$19.2 million	$900,000 over 3.5 years
Minnesota State Arts Board (MSAB) Executive Director: Robert Booker Park Square Court 400 Sibley Street, Suite 200 St. Paul, MN 55101	$2.66 (9)	$13.7 million	$1.1 million over 4.5 years
Mississippi Arts Commission (MSAC) Executive Director: Timothy Hedgepeth 239 North Lamar Street, Suite 207 Jackson, MS 39201	$1.15 (26)	$3.3 million	$700,000 over 3 years

Agency	Per Capita Spending (Rank)[a]	Total Revenue[b]	START Grant
Montana Arts Council (MAC) Executive Director: Arlynn Fishbaugh P.O. Box 202201 316 North Park Avenue, Room 252 Helena, MT 59620–2201	$0.32 (55)	$1.7 million	$500,000 over 5 years
New Jersey State Council on the Arts (NJSCA) Executive Director: David Miller P.O. Box 306 225 West State Street Trenton, NJ 08625–0306	$2.63 (10)	$22.9 million	$900,000 over 5 years
North Carolina Arts Council (NCAC) Executive Director: Mary Regan Department of Cultural Resources Jenkins House 221 East Lane Street Raleigh, NC 27699–4632	$0.97 (31)	$8.5 million	$1 million over 4 years
Ohio Arts Council (OAC) Executive Director: Wayne Lawson 727 East Main Street Columbus, OH 43205	$1.39 (20)	$17.4 million	$1.1 million over 3 years
South Carolina Arts Commission (SCAC) Executive Director: Suzette Surkamer 1800 Gervais Street Columbia, SC 29201	$1.35 (22)	$6.4 million	$800,000 over 5 years
Washington State Arts Commission (WSAC) Executive Director: Kris Tucker P.O. Box 42675 234 East 8th Avenue Olympia, WA 98504–2675	$0.45 (52)	$4.6 million	$500,000 over 5 years

SOURCE: NASAA, 2001; Wallace-Reader's Digest Funds, 2001.

[a] Including line items and is in U.S. dollars; rank is out of all 56 SAAs.

[b] Rounded to the nearest $100,000. Revenue sources are legislative appropriations (including line items), NEA grants, and other state funds.

APPENDIX B

Summary Information for 43 Non-START State and Jurisdictional Arts Agencies, FY 2001

Agency	Per Capita Spending (Rank)[a]	Total Revenue in $ millions
Alabama	$1.38 (21)	$7.5
Alaska	$0.73 (36)	$1.1
American Samoa	$0.64 (42)	$0.3
Arkansas	$0.49 (48)	$2.2
Colorado	$0.44 (53)	$3.8
Delaware	$2.11 (15)	$2.2
District of Columbia	$3.32 (5)	$3.4
Florida	$2.31 (13)	$37.5
Georgia	$0.59 (46)	$5.3
Guam	$3.22 (6)	$0.7
Hawaii	$4.96 (1)	$6.5
Idaho	$0.74 (35)	$1.4
Illinois	$1.59 (18)	$20.4
Indiana	$0.63 (43)	$4.4
Iowa	$0.58 (47)	$2.7
Kansas	$0.61 (45)	$2.1
Louisiana	$1.10 (28)	$5.6
Maine	$0.63 (44)	$1.3
Maryland	$2.39 (12)	$13.4
Michigan	$2.60 (11)	$26.4
Missouri	$2.14 (14)	$12.5
Nebraska	$0.85 (33)	$2.7
Nevada	$0.67 (39)	$2.0
New Hampshire	$0.48 (51)	$1.1
New Mexico	$1.06 (29)	$2.8
New York	$2.99 (7)	$57.4
North Dakota	$0.66 (41)	$0.9
Northern Marianas	$3.91 (4)	$0.5
Oklahoma	$1.23 (25)	$5.2
Oregon	$0.48 (50)	$2.1
Pennsylvania	$1.14 (27)	$14.7
Puerto Rico	$4.71 (2)	$26.9
Rhode Island	$1.67 (17)	$1.9
South Dakota	$0.68 (38)	$1.1
Tennessee	$0.41 (54)	$5.5
Texas	$0.23 (56)	$5.4

Agency	Per Capita Spending (Rank)[a]	Total Revenue in $ millions
Utah	$1.24 (24)	$4.2
Vermont	$0.93 (32)	$1.7
Virgin Islands	$1.54 (19)	$0.4
Virginia	$0.66 (40)	$5.2
West Virginia	$1.30 (23)	$3.9
Wisconsin	$0.48 (49)	$3.1
Wyoming	$0.71 (37)	$1.0

SOURCE: NASAA, 2001

[a] Includes line items and is in U.S. dollars; rank is out of all 56 SAAs.

[b] Rounded to the nearest $100,000. Revenue sources are legislative appropriations (including line items), NEA grants, and other state funds.

Bibliography

AAFRC Trust for Philanthropy, *Giving USA: The Annual Report for Philanthropy*, New York: AFFRC Trust for Philanthropy, 2000.

Adams, Don, and Arlene Goldbard, "Comprehensive Cultural Policy for the State of California," unpublished document commissioned for the State of California, December 1978. Available at http://www.wwcd.org/.

Adams, Don, and Arlene Goldbard, *Cultural Policy in U.S. History*, essay adpated from unpublished 1986 manuscript, 1995. Available at http://www.wwcd.org/.

Addison, Lynn R., "Beads, Bandannas, and Blue Jeans: The Arts Council Only a Governor Can Love," *California Journal*, Vol. 7, September 1976, pp. 317–319.

Americans for the Arts, *Local Arts Agency Facts: Fiscal Year 2000*, Washington, D.C., August 2001.

Arian, Edward, *The Unfulfilled Promise: Public Subsidy of the Arts in America*, Philadelphia: Temple University Press, 1989.

Association of Performing Arts Presenters, *1995 Profile of Member Organizations*, Washington DC: APAP, 1995.

Baumol, William J., and William G. Bowen, "On the Performing Arts: The Anatomy of Their Economic Problems," *American Economic Review*, Vol. 55, No. 1, March 1965, pp. 495–502.

Baumol, William J., and William G. Bowen, *Performing Arts—The Economic Dilemma: A Study of Problems Common to Theater, Opera, Music and Dance*, New York: The Twentieth Century Fund, 1966.

Biddle, Livingston, *Our Government and the Arts: A Perspective from the Inside*, New York: ACA Books, 1988.

Bourdieu, Pierre, *Distinction*, translated by Richard Nice, Cambridge, MA: Harvard University Press, 1994.

Brustein, Robert, "The Decline of High Culture," *The New Republic*, Vol. 217, No. 18, 3 November 1997, p. 29.

Brustein, Robert, "Requiem," *The New Republic*, 27 March 2000.

California Arts Council (CAC), *2001 Public Opinion Survey*, Sacramento, CA: CAC, 2001. Available at http://www.cac.ca.gov/library/publications.cfm.

Callan, Patrick, "Coping with Recession: Public Policy, Economic Downturns and Higher Education," Research Report 02-2, San Jose, CA: National Center for Public Policy and Higher Education, February 2002. Available at http://www.highereducation.org/reports/reports_center.shtml#2002.

Campbell, Mary Schmidt, "A New Mission for the NEA," *The Drama Review*, Vol. 42, No. 4, Winter 1998, pp. 5–9. (Reprinted in Gigi Bradford, Michael Gary, and Glenn Wallach, eds., *The Politics of Culture: Policy Perspectives for Individuals, Institutions, and Communities,* New York: The New Press, 2000, pp. 141–146.)

Cohen, Randy, "Local Government Support of Arts and Culture," *The Journal of Arts Management, Law, and Society*, Vol. 32, No. 3, Fall 2002, pp. 206–184.

Conforti, Michael, "Expanding the Canon of Art Collecting," *Museum News*, September/October 1989, pp. 36–40.

Cummings, Milton C., Jr., "Government and the Arts: An Overview," in Stephen Benedict, ed., *Public Money and the Muse*, New York: W.W. Norton, 1991, pp. 31–79.

Danto, Arthur C., "Museums and the Thirsty Millions," in Arthur M. Melzer, Jerry Weinberger, and M. Richard Zinman, eds., *Democracy and the Arts*, Ithaca, NY: Cornell University Press, 1999.

DiMaggio, Paul J., "Decentralization of Arts Funding from the Federal Government to the States," in Stephen Benedict, ed., *Public Money and the Muse*, New York: W.W. Norton, 1991, pp. 216–56.

DiMaggio, Paul J., and Becky Pettit, "Public Opinion and Political Vulnerability: Why Has the National Endowment for the Arts Been Such an Attractive Target?", Princeton University Center for Arts and Cultural Policy Studies Working Paper No. 7, January 1999.

DiMaggio, Paul J., and Michael Useem, "Social Class and Arts Consumption: The Origins and Consequences of Class Differences in Exposure to the Arts in America," *Theory and Society*, Vol. 5, No. 1, Spring 1978, pp. 141–161.

Dworkin, Dennis, "State Advocacy and the Arts: A Historical Overview," *Journal of Arts Management and Law,* Vol. 21, No. 3, Fall 1991, pp. 199–214.

Eddy, Junius, "Government, the Arts, and Ghetto Youth," *Public Administration Review,* July/August 1970, pp. 399–408.

Filicko, Therese, "What Do We Need to Know About Culture?" Occasional Paper No. 5, Arts Policy and Administration Program, Ohio State University, 1997.

Galligan, Ann M., "The Politicization of Peer Review Panels at the NEA," in Judith Huggins Balfe, ed., *Paying the Piper: Causes and Consequences of Arts Patronage*, Urbana, IL: University of Illinois Press, 1993, pp. 254–270.

Goldbard, Arlene, "The Awful Truth in Five Acts," author's preface to *Comprehensive Cultural Policy for the State of California*, San Francisco, CA, 30 December 1978. Available at http://www.wwcd.org.

Grantmakers in the Arts, *A Snapshot: Foundation Grants to Arts and Culture, 1999,* Seattle, WA: Grantmakers in the Arts, 2001.

Hansmann, Henry, "Nonprofit Enterprise in the Performing Arts," *Bell Journal of Economics*, Vol.12, No. 2, 1981, pp. 341–361.

Harris, John S., "Arts Councils: A Survey and Analysis," *Public Administration Review*, July/August 1970, pp. 387–399.

Harris, Neil, "Public Subsidies and American Art," presentation at the October 1995 Grantmakers in the Arts Conference, Eureka, CA, reprinted in *Grantmakers in the Arts Newletter*, Vol. 7, Spring 1996.

Horowitz, Harold, "The Federal and State Partnership in the Support of Culture in the U.S.A.," *Journal of Cultural Economics* Vol. 10, No. 2, December 1986, pp. 1–26.

Izumi, Lance, "Creating Cultural Consumers," in *Cultural Policy in the West*, Denver, CO: Western State Arts Federation, 23–24 September 1999, 16–18.

Jaggi, Maya, "Blowing Up a Storm," *The Guardian*, 25 January 2003.

Jazz at Lincoln Center, "Jazz at Lincoln Center," public relations document, n.d. Available at http://www.jazzatlincolncenter.org/jalc/jalcbio.pdf.

Joseph C. Burke and Associates, *Funding Public Colleges and Universities for Performance: Popularity, Problems, and Prospects*, New York: Rockefeller Institute, 2002.

Kammen, Michael, "Culture and the State in America," *Journal of American History*, Vol. 83, December 1996, pp. 791–834. (Reprinted in Gigi Bradford, Michael Gary, and Glenn Wallach, eds., *The Politics of Culture: Policy Perspectives for Individuals, Institutions, and Communities,* New York: The New Press, 2000, pp. 114–140.)

Keller, Anthony S., "Arts Policy, Cultural Diversity, and the New Century," in David B. Pankratz and Valerie B. Morris, eds., *The Future of the Arts: Public Policy and Arts Research*, New York: Praeger, 1990.

Kettl, Donald F., *Reinventing Government: A Fifth-Year Report Card*, Center for Public Management Report CPM 98–1, Washington, D.C.: Brookings Institution, September 1998.

Kreidler, John, "Leverage Lost: Evolution in the Nonprofit Arts Ecosystem," *Journal of Arts Management, Law and Society*, Vol. 26, No. 2, Summer 1999, pp. 79–100.

Kupcha, Dorothy A., "Tale of the Dolphin Drum: How the Arts Council Shed the 'Weirdo' Image," *California Journal*, Vol. 9, September 1979, pp. 318–320.

Larson, Gary O., *The Reluctant Patron: The United States Government and the Arts, 1943–65*, Philadelphia: University of Pennsylvania Press, 1983.

Larson, Gary O., *American Canvas,* Washington, D.C.: NEA, 1997.

Levine, Lawrence W., *The Opening of the American Mind*, Boston: Beacon Press, 1996.

Levine, Lawrence W., *Highbrow Lowbrow: The Emergence of Cultural Hierarchy in America*, Cambridge, MA: Harvard University Press, 1998.

Love, Jeffrey, "Sorting Out Our Roles: The State Arts Agencies and the National Endowment for the Arts," *Journal of Arts Management, Law and Society*, Vol. 21, No. 3, Fall 1991, pp. 215–226.

Love, Jeffrey, and Bramble C. Klipple, *Arts Participation and Race/Ethnicity: An Analysis of 1982, 1985, and 1992 SPPA Surveys*, Washington, D.C.: NEA, 1995.

Mark, Charles Christopher, *Reluctant Bureaucrats: The Struggle to Establish the National Endowment for the Arts*, Dubuque, IA: Kendall/Hunt Publishing, 1990.

Marquis, Alice Goldfarb, *Art Lessons: Learning from the Rise and Fall of Public Arts Funding*, New York: Basic Books, 1995.

Massachusetts Cultural Council, "A Brief History of the Massachusetts Cultural Council," unpublished draft document, n.d.

Mattern, Mark, and Katherine Kratz, "Ohio Arts Council/Ohio Arts Presenters Network 2001 Faith-Based Institution Tour: Final Report," unpublished evaluation conducted for the Ohio Arts Council, 31 May 2002.

McCarthy, Kevin F., and Kimberly Jinnett, *A New Framework for Building Participation in the Arts*, MR-1323-WRDF, Santa Monica, CA: RAND Corporation, 2001.

McCarthy, Kevin F., Arthur Brooks, Julia Lowell, and Laura Zakaras, *The Performing Arts in a New Era*, MR-1367-PCT, Santa Monica, CA: RAND Corporation, 2001.

Montana Arts Council, *FY 2001–2006 Strategic Plan*, Executive Summary, n.d. Available at http://www.art.state.mt.us/about/about_strategicexsum.htm.

Moore, Mark H., *Creating Public Value: Strategic Management in Government*, Cambridge, MA: Harvard University Press, 1995.

Moore, Mark H., "Managing for Value: Organizational Strategy in For-Profit, Nonprofit, and Governmental Organizations," *Nonprofit and Voluntary Sector Quarterly*, Vol. 29, No. 1, Supplement, 2000, pp. 183–204.

Mulcahy, Kevin V., "The State Arts Agency: An Overview of Cultural Federalism in the United States," *The Journal of Arts Management, Law, and Society*, Vol. 32, No. 1, Spring 2002, pp. 67–80.

National Assembly of State Arts Agencies (NASAA), *Decentralization Strategies in State Arts Agencies: Profile Breakout*, Washington, D.C.: NASAA, August 1995.

National Assembly of State Arts Agencies (NASAA), *A State Arts Agency Performance Measurement Toolkit*, Washington, D.C.: NASAA, November 1996.

National Assembly of State Arts Agencies (NASAA), *State Arts Agency Public Funding Sourcebook 1966–2000*, Washington, D.C.: NASAA, 2000.

National Assembly of State Arts Agencies (NASAA), "State Arts Agency Staffing Trends," *Research Brief* 2/1, Washington, D.C.: NASAA, 2001.

National Assembly of State Arts Agencies (NASAA), *Legislative Appropriations Annual Survey Fiscal Year 2003*, Washington, D.C.: NASAA, December 2002.

National Assembly of State Arts Agencies (NASAA), *Legislative Appropriations Annual Survey Fiscal Year 2004*, Washington, D.C.: NASAA, October 2003.

National Assembly of State Arts Agencies (NASAA), "The State Perspective on Federal Support for the Arts," unpublished talking points, n.d.

National Assembly of State Arts Agencies (NASAA) and National Endowment for the Arts (NEA), *State Arts Agency Funding and Grantmaking*, Washington, D.C.: NASAA and NEA, February 2001.

National Conference of State Legislatures, *State Budget & Tax Actions 2003,* Preliminary Report: Executive Summary, Denver, CO: National Conference of State Legislatures, 2003.

National Endowment for the Arts (NEA), *State Arts Agencies in 1974: Present and Accounted For*, Research Division Report No. 8, Washington, D.C.: NEA, April 1978.

National Endowment for the Arts (NEA), *Census Reports 28% Increase in Number of Nonprofit Theaters: 1982–1987*, Research Division Note No. 45, Washington, D.C.: NEA, September 30, 1993a.

National Endowment for the Arts (NEA), *Census Reports 18% Increase in Nonprofit Dance Groups: 1982–1987*, Research Division Note No. 46, Washington, D.C.: NEA, 30 September 1993b.

National Endowment for the Arts (NEA), *Census Reports 30% Increase in Nonprofit Classical Music Groups: 1982–1987*, Research Division Note No. 47, Washington, D.C.: NEA, 30 September 1993c.

National Endowment for the Arts (NEA), *Census Reports 6% Increase in Art Museums and Art Galleries: 1982–1987*, Research Division Note No. 48, Washington, D.C.: NEA, 30 September 1993d.

National Endowment for the Arts (NEA), *Annual Report 1999*, Washington, D.C.: NEA, 2000.

National Endowment for the Arts (NEA), *Guide to the NEA*, Washington, D.C.: NEA, January 2003. Available at http://arts.endow.gov/learn/NEAGuide/Contents.html.

Netzer, Dick, *The Subsidized Muse: Public Support for the Arts in the United States*, Cambridge, UK: Cambridge University Press, 1978.

Ohio Arts Council, *The State of the Arts Report: A Blueprint for Ohio's Communities*, Columbus, OH: Ohio Arts Council, 2001. Available at http://www.ohiosoar.org.

Osborne, David, and Ted Gaebler, *Reinventing Government: How the Entrepreneurial Spirit Is Transforming the Public Sector*, New York: Penguin Books, 1993.

Pankratz, David B., *Multiculturalism and Public Arts Policy*, Westport, CT: Bergin and Garvey, 1993.

Robinson, John P., *Arts Participation in America: 1982–1992*, Washington, D.C.: NEA, 1993.

Robinson, John P., and Therese Filicko, "American Public Opinion About the Arts and Culture: The Unceasing War with Philistia," in Joni Cherbo and Margaret Wyszomirski, eds., *The Public Life of the Arts in America*, New Brunswick, NJ: Rutgers University Press, 2000.

Robinson, John P., et al., *Public Participation in the Arts: Final Report on the 1982 Survey*, Washington, D.C.: NEA, 1985.

Rockefeller Brothers Fund, *The Performing Arts: Problems and Prospects*, Rockefeller Panel Report No. 7, New York: McGraw Hill, 1965.

Savage, James D., "Populism, Decentralization, and Arts Policy in California," *Administration and Society*, Vol. 20, No. 4, February 1989, pp. 446–464.

Schuster, J. Mark Davidson, *The Audience for American Art Museums*, Research Report No. 23, Washington, D.C.: NEA, 1991.

Schwarz, Samuel, *Growth of Arts and Cultural Organizations in the Decade of the 1970s*, NEA-PC-80-29, Washington, D.C.: National Endowment for the Arts, December 1983.

Scitovsky, Tibor, "What's Wrong with the Arts Is What's Wrong with Society," *American Economic Review*, May 1972, pp. 1–19.

Scott, Mel, "The Federal-State Partnership in the Arts," *Public Administration Review*, July-August 1970, pp. 376–386.

Starker, Melissa, "Creative Accounting," *Columbus Alive,* 13 December 2001. Available at http://www.columbusalive.com/2001/20011213/.

Urice, John K., "The Future of the State Arts Agency Movement in the 1990s: Decline and Effect," *Journal of Arts Management, Law, and Society*, Vol. 22, No. 1, Spring 1992, pp. 19–32.

U.S. Congress, House Committee on Education and Labor, *Aid to Fine Arts: Hearing Before the Select Subcommittee on Education on H.R. 4172, H.R. 4174 and Related Bills to Aid the Fine Arts in the United States*, 87th Congress, 1st Session, Washington, D.C., 15 May 1961.

U.S. Congress, Senate Committee on Labor and Public Welfare, *Government and the Arts: Hearing Before A Special Subcommittee on Labor and Public Welfare on S.741, S.785, and S. 1250*, 87th Congress, 2nd Session, Washington, D.C., 29–31 August 1962.

Wallace-Reader's Digest Funds, "Arts Grants," March 2001. Available at http://www.wallace-funds.org/frames/framesetnews.htm.

Washington State Arts Commission (WSAC), *General Guidelines, Policies and Procedures FY2004: Subsection Applies to Project Support Program, Cooperative Partnerships, Institutional Support Program, Organizational Support Program*, Olympia, WA: WSAC, February 2003.

Washington State Arts Commission (WSAC), "Grants to Organizations: How Grants Are Awarded," n.d. Available at http://www.arts.wa.gov/.

Willoughby, Katherine G., and Julia Melkers, "Performance-Based Budgeting Requirements in State Government," Fiscal Research Policy Brief No. 7, Andrew Young School of Policy Studies, Georgia State University, June 1998.

Wooden, Cecelia K., "Who Is KCA? Our History," Louisville, KY: Kentucky Citizens for the Arts, 2001. Available at http://www.kyartsadvocates.com/whois.htm.

Wyszomirski, Margaret Jane, "Controversies in Arts Policymaking," in Kevin Mulcahy and C. Richard Swaim, eds., *Public Policy and the Arts*, Boulder, CO: Westview Press, 1982, pp. 11–32.

Wyszomirski, Margaret Jane, "Philanthropy and Culture: Patterns, Context, and Change," in Charles Clotfelter and Thomas Erlich, eds., *Philanthropy and the Nonprofit Sector in a Changing America*, Bloomington: Indiana University Press, 1999, pp. 461–480.

Zeigler, Joseph Wesley, *Arts in Crisis: The National Endowment for the Arts Versus America*, Chicago: A Capella Books, 1994.